EARNED

Why Brilliant, Hardworking
People Stay Broke
(And the Framework That Changes It)

Duemand L. Edwards
with Robert T. Vaughn

Seeds4Wealth Publication

ISBN: 979-8-234-08085-1

Library of Congress Control Number: 2026911937

Published by Seeds4Wealth Publishing

Printed in the United States of America

Editorial Credit: Developmental editing and editorial guidance by Rob Peace. The authors extend sincere gratitude for his exceptional editorial insight, precision, and commitment to excellence throughout the development of this work.

For more information, visit www.seeds4wealth.org

Contents

INTRODUCTION

Wealth Was Never Just About Money

Before anything else, let's begin by smashing a grand misconception that's been standing in your way: The problem isn't your work ethic. In fact, it never was.

You've been showing up, doing your absolute best, and even carrying the weight of others while making it all stretch. And still, wealth has always felt *just* out of your reach. Not because you weren't capable—and certainly not because you didn't care—but because no one handed you the blueprint.

What does that mean in simple terms? It means that wealth has always been written in a language that most of us were never taught to read. That language includes things like 'ownership,' 'leverage,' 'compounding'—concepts that shape outcomes quietly over time. Most people aren't introduced to them early, and by the time they encounter them, they're already playing catch-up.

You're not delusional if you've always felt like the rules keep changing or that the game wasn't made for you to win; it's how the system was quietly designed. So, if you've constantly felt behind despite doing "everything right," this book will help you conquer the obstacles you've never been able to bypass.

But it's important to note from the outset that this is a book about reclamation, not blame. Wealth isn't just reserved for the lucky, the connected, or the "born into it." Wealth is *built*, and it's built on a foundation of clarity, systems, courage, and values.

We created this book because we grew tired of seeing brilliant people remaining stuck. Weary of watching exhaustion attract praise while ambition gets punished. Frustrated with watching our communities wait for permission to rise. So, we built what those communities (and you) needed: a framework to make wealth make sense.

A Moment of Truth

I remember the night I realized I was done pretending I was okay. I'd just paid all my bills, and there was $73 left in my account. I didn't have any savings, and definitely no backup plan. In my tank was just enough gas to get to work the next day.

I wasn't reckless or lazy. I'd actually been working hard. But I was trapped in a cycle where survival was the reward, and anything beyond that felt like a luxury I hadn't earned.

The shame completely broke me. Shame that I was supposed to have it figured out by now. Shame that I didn't even know what questions to ask. Shame that I was making everything look okay while it was all quietly falling apart.

That night, I stopped performing success and started rebuilding it on my own terms. Because what I realized is that wealth isn't about a number. It's about peace. It's about power and the ability to choose. And I was finally ready to choose differently, even if it meant *unlearning* everything I thought I knew in order to get there.

The Distinction That Changes Everything

That lowly $73 in my bank account taught me something that no budgeting app or motivational speech had ever told me: that every decision I'd ever made with money—every single one—was a survival decision.

Not a bad decision. Not a lazy decision. A *survival decision.*

Think about what that means for a moment. When I avoided opening my bank statements, that was a survival decision, the nervous system protecting itself from information that felt threatening. When I gave money to family members I couldn't afford to give to, that was a survival decision to protect the relationships that had always been my real safety net. When I spent a little extra at the end of a hard week just to feel like I'd earned something, that was a survival decision; it was emotional relief in the absence of anything else. When I didn't open an investment account because investing felt like something "other people" did, that was a survival decision not to risk what little I had on something that felt uncertain and foreign.

None of those decisions were irrational. The conditions they came from (real scarcity, real instability, real absence of financial education or safety nets) had all made sense. The problem was that I was still making those decisions long after the conditions had started to change. My income had grown and my circumstances had shifted, but my financial operating system was still running on the same code it always had: survive first and build later, all while praying that "later" eventually showed up.

This is what I know now, and also what this book is built around: *Every financial decision you'll ever make is either a survival decision or a wealth decision.* The difference between them?

Survival decisions protect what you have.

Wealth decisions build what you don't have yet.

Both matter, because you need survival decisions when your survival is genuinely at stake. But brilliant, hardworking people get stuck when they keep making survival decisions out of habit, fear, or an identity that hasn't caught up with their circumstances. And they get stuck because no one ever handed them the lens to see the difference.

That lens is what this book delivers. The ELITE Principles are the framework for building wealth, but underneath every principle is this same distinction in a different form. Elevating your mindset is learning to recognize a survival belief before it makes a wealth decision for you. Leveraging what you know is the shift from undercharging out of survival instinct to pricing from a position of real value.

Investing with intention is the move from "let's protect what little I have" to "let's grow what I have." Tidying your finances is replacing the chaos of survival management with the order of wealth management. Extending the legacy is the moment you stop building just for your own security and start building for what outlasts you.

Every chapter in this book teaches you to make a different kind of decision, not out of shame or because they were wrong (they weren't), but because you're no longer in the same conditions that made them necessary.

And you deserve a financial life that reflects who you're becoming, not who you once had to be.

The ELITE Principles

This trademarked framework is value-based and repeatable, and it's designed to help you build wealth on your own terms. Here's how it works:

E	**Elevate Your Mindset** *Reclaim your beliefs, challenge what you were taught, and step into the version of yourself that wealth was waiting for.*
L	**Leverage What You Know** *Your skills, your story, and your experience are all assets. Let's put them to work.*
I	**Invest with Intention** *Forget complexity. Wealth grows through aligned, consistent, real-life investing. Yes, even for beginners.*
T	**Tidy & Tune Your Finances** *Clarity over chaos, and rhythm over restriction. Together, we'll build you a system that works for you, not against you.*
E	**Extend the Legacy** *The goal isn't just to attain wealth for yourself and stop there. It's to pass it on through structure, knowledge, and generosity (albeit with boundaries, but we'll cover those as well).*

This all comes down to building a stable life, not necessarily a perfect one. A spacious one in which your money moves in the direction of your values. This is your reminder that you don't have to shrink to feel safe. You don't have to earn rest through burnout. Your strategy, and your story, can be the beginning of a new kind of legacy.

Wealth isn't a fantasy, nor is it out of reach or just for "everyone else." You don't need luck. What you need is a lens shift to realize that whatever's ahead isn't given.

It's earned.

Before We Start

This isn't the kind of book you read once, highlight a few lines here and there, and leave it on the shelf. EARNED is a book you *work* through. Read a chapter a week, or one principle a month. At the end of most chapters, you'll find journal prompts that we've called *Course Correction Reflections*. These give you an opportunity to pause, reflect, and reframe with honesty, but the prompts are only effective if you answer them truthfully. Don't skip these, because the writing is where the shift happens.

And when you can, share your work with someone else. Teaching what you're learning out loud helps you embody it faster, and it gives others permission to start, too.

The Myths That Brought You Here

But before we dive into the framework, it'll be helpful to name the misinformation that's probably already in the room with you. These are the 10 most common myths that keep people financially stuck, not because they're lazy or irresponsible but because these ideas were handed to them as truth. See how many of them you recognize, then get ready to leave them behind. There's actually an 11th myth at the end of the list, which is the most crucial one of all. And if you believe in this myth, all the others are essentially guaranteed to follow.

Myth #1: "Money is evil."

Truth: Money magnifies what's already in you. In the right hands, it creates freedom, opportunity, and impact.

Myth #2: "Debt is always bad."

Truth: Debt is a tool. When used strategically, it can unlock ownership and acceleration. When misused, it becomes a trap.

Myth #3: "Investing is only for the rich."

Truth: Investing is how people *become* rich. Waiting until you "have more" ensures that you'll always have less.

Myth #4: "I'm just not good with money."

Truth: Money is a skill, not a personality trait. Skills can be learned, practiced, and mastered.

Myth #5: "Multiple streams mean multiple hustles."

Truth: Wealthy people don't chase more jobs; they build systems. True streams flow from assets, not exhaustion.

Myth #6: "If I work harder, I'll finally get ahead."

Truth: Effort matters, but strategy multiplies. Hustle without direction just burns time and energy.

Myth #7: "Saving is the goal."

Truth: Saving is a starting line, not a finish line. Ownership and investing are what build wealth that grows.

Myth #8: "I can catch up later."

Truth: Later never comes. Wealth is built in daily, disciplined steps. And it starts today.

Myth #9: "Wealth is about what you keep."

Truth: True wealth is about what you build and extend to others. Remember that legacy outlives accumulation.

Myth #10: "I need permission to start."

Truth: No one is coming to hand you your future. You already have what you need to get started. So, get started.

But the biggest myth of all? That wealth is out of reach.

Truth: Wealth is already within your grasp, as long as you're willing to shift your mindset, take small steps, and keep building. Because wealth is about choosing. It's not about being chosen.

Before you continue reading, make three commitments with yourself:

> *I will read with honesty, not performance.*
>
> *I will engage with at least one journal prompt per principle.*
>
> *I will take one action, however small, from each chapter. I'll write it down, sign it, and date it.*

These three commitments will be the catalyst for the change you're seeking, because the big shifts in your life occur when you take action. If everything remains in theory, everything stays the same.

Let's begin.

PART I

ELEVATE Your Mindset

Unlearn, Reframe & See Yourself As Capable of Wealth

CHAPTER ONE

Unlearn the Lies

> *The first step to wealth is rewriting the story you were told. If you don't learn to unlearn, you'll keep reliving someone else's story instead of writing your own.*

Before we cover the topics of earning more, investing better, or building a legacy, we need to address something that gets in the way of all of it: the lies. Not the obvious scams or schemes, but the quiet lies. The ones that were passed down to you with love, wrapped in the best intentions from people who were also just trying to survive. These mistruths settled into your mind so early and so deeply that they don't even feel like beliefs anymore. They feel like facts.

Whether you realize it or not, your entire relationship with money is shaped by beliefs you never actually chose. You inherited them from your parents, your church, your neighborhood, and your culture—from every person who ever said something about money in your presence when you were too young to question it. And if you don't go back and examine those beliefs, they'll keep running your financial life long after you've outgrown everything else about the world you came from.

So that's our starting point. We're not beginning with budget planning or investment accounts, but with the stories that got to you first.

The First Lie: Money Is Evil

You've heard variations of this your whole life: *Money changes people. Rich people are greedy. You don't need much, just enough to get by.* These things were said in kitchens and church pews and on front porches by people who genuinely believed them and genuinely loved you. That's what makes this lie so hard to shake. It doesn't feel like a lie; it feels like wisdom and humility.

But what it actually does is make you afraid of the very thing you need. When you're taught that money corrupts, that wanting more makes you greedy, and that ambition is something to be tamed, your spirit starts pulling away from financial growth before you even consciously decide to. You don't pursue opportunities because some part of you believes that doing so makes you a certain kind of person. You stay comfortable because comfort has been coded as righteousness.

The truth is that money is neutral. It's not moral or immoral on its own. At its most basic, it's a resource. And like any resource, it amplifies what's already within the person who's holding it. If you're generous, money allows you to be more generous. If you're community-minded, money gives that instinct more reach. The people who've used wealth to do harm weren't corrupted by the money. The money just gave them more room to be who they already were. And this matters, because the belief that money is evil isn't protecting you from anything. It's just keeping you broke and disguising itself as virtue.

The Second Lie: Debt Is Bad, Full Stop

Cut up your cards. Pay it off or don't touch it. Debt is the enemy. You've heard some versions of these too, and to be fair, they didn't come from nowhere. Predatory lending is real, and so are credit card traps. There are entire industries built around keeping certain communities in cycles of high-interest debt, and the damage they've done is generational.

But the belief that *all* debt is dangerous? That's fear that became overgeneralized into a rule. And the problem with that rule is that it keeps you from learning something that wealthy people understand from the beginning: that debt is actually one of the primary tools used to build wealth.

Most of us were never taught how interest actually works, how it can either erode your savings from underneath you or compound your returns over time. We were never taught the difference between debt that *costs* you money and debt that *makes* you money. We were never shown how business credit works, or how the same mechanism that traps people in payday loan cycles is the exact same mechanism—used differently—that built fortunes. We were just warned to stay away from it entirely, to be scared off and kept in the dark. This book isn't here to glorify debt. There *is* bad debt, and we'll talk about how to recognize it, but truly understanding debt simply isn't optional if you want to build wealth.

The Third Lie: You'll Never Be Rich Unless You Were Born Into It

This one is sneaky because it's partly true, and partial truths are the hardest lies to let go of. Generational wealth is real, and the playing field isn't equal. There are people who start life with resources, networks, and safety nets that most of us will never have access to, and pretending otherwise would be dishonest. The system that created those advantages was built deliberately, and it's kept certain people out just as deliberately.

But most wealth, even among people who appear to have always had it, was built with decisions and systems. It was a different relationship with money: a willingness to invest instead of just spend, to own instead of just earn, and to think beyond the next paycheck. Those things are learnable, and they always have been. The only reason they felt unavailable to you is that no one in your immediate world was practicing them, and no one handed you the language to even name what you were missing.

You need structure, not a trust fund or a lucky break. You need a strategy that isn't built around *waiting* for one. The system being real doesn't cancel out your agency. Both things are true, and reclaiming one doesn't require you to pretend the other doesn't exist.

The Fourth Lie: The System Makes It Pointless to Try

Many of us have been financially gatekept for generations, from redlining to underfunded schools, from predatory lenders to hiring discrimination, and from the racial wealth gap to the ways that financial education has historically been distributed unevenly along racial and economic lines. This is documented and real. If you've spent your life feeling like the rules keep changing and the game wasn't designed for you to win, you weren't imagining it.

The lie, however, is that it's therefore pointless to try—that because the starting line was moved, the race can't be run, and that because the table was built to exclude you, there's no point in building your own.

You were never the problem. You weren't lazy, irresponsible, or "bad with money." You were misinformed and underserved by systems designed to keep wealth concentrated. Not only that, but you were told, in countless ways, that your situation was your own fault. That's the deepest and most damaging lie of all, and now you know where it came from.

But knowing this changes everything, because it means the solution isn't fixing some kind of flaw in yourself; it's replacing bad information with *better* information. It's reclaiming the agency that was always yours, just never named. That's what this book will remedy.

Research consistently shows that adults who didn't receive financial education growing up carry that gap into their financial decisions for decades, not because of lack of effort or intelligence, but because the mental models they're working from were never updated. The biggest wealth gap isn't in the bank account. It's in the information. And that's a gap that can be closed.

Each of the four lies above served the same function: they kept you making survival decisions, because that's what misinformation does. It programs your financial operating system for scarcity. Then that operating system runs quietly in the background, making decisions you think to be rational but are actually just made out of habit. Unlearning the lies is the first step toward recognizing which decisions you're making from survival mode, and which ones you're finally ready to make from somewhere more informed.

Course Correction Reflections

Q1

What beliefs about money did you grow up with, and where did each one come from?

Q2

When you look at your financial decisions today, which of those inherited beliefs are still quietly running the show?

CHAPTER TWO

Stop Playing Small with Your Story

> *You weren't born to shrink. You were born to stretch.*

Once you start unlearning the lies, another truth surfaces: You've been playing small. Not because you weren't built for more, but because small felt safe and manageable. You convinced yourself that shrinking was strategic, that dreaming big was risky, and that reaching higher than what felt comfortable was irresponsible. But playing small is stagnation in disguise, not wisdom.

I remember the first time someone asked me what I actually wanted. Not what I was settling for, and not what seemed realistic, but what I genuinely wanted my life to look like. I almost didn't have an answer, because I'd spent so long editing my dreams down to fit what I thought was possible for someone like me. That conversation cracked something open. I realized I'd been making myself smaller out of self-protection. If I never named the real goal, I could never really fail at it. But the cost of that protection was my potential.

Small Thinking Isn't Humble. It's a Trap.

Here's what most of us were taught: modest goals are admirable, wanting more is greedy, and ambition is something to be tamed. These ideas sound virtuous, but they're not. They're the invisible bars of a cage that looks like common sense.

The people who break cycles and build legacy don't play it safe. They stretch. They pursue goals that scare them and they move forward, even without a full blueprint. Starting small is fine, but *staying* small isn't strategy. It's just self-doubt with good branding.

You're allowed to want more income, more ownership, and more clarity. You're allowed to outgrow environments that celebrate your smallness. Bigger rooms to step into, bolder goals to achieve, higher standards to live by, a different financial reality than the one you came from… These aren't arrogant aspirations. They're alignment. You're remembering who you are, and that's the complete opposite of being unrealistic.

Playing Small Has a Price Tag

Most people don't say the following out loud, but that doesn't stop it from being true: Playing small is expensive, both emotionally and financially. When you underestimate your value, you underprice your work. When you shrink your vision, you shrink your earning potential with it. The person who charges $50 for something worth $500 is making a survival decision. Keeping the price low feels safer than risking rejection with the number that's actually indicative of its true value. But that gap between what you charge and what you're worth compounds over time, just like debt. Every year of underpricing is a year of wealth you didn't build.

This applies to every negotiation, every raise conversation, and every time you said yes to a role that paid less than you knew you deserved because having "something" felt safer than asking for what you were worth. Playing small has a running total, and at some point you have to decide whether the safety is worth the cost.

Define the Mountaintop. Then Move.

You don't need to know every step or have all the resources. You just need to name the vision. Then take one bold step, even if it's steep or imperfect. Your vision will evolve, and so it should. You're allowed to grow. But don't stay at the base of the mountain pretending it isn't there.

You may not have capital or connections yet. But you *do* have value. And when you align your vision with others who recognize that value, you unlock possibility. Big dreams aren't built in isolation; they're built in community, through collaboration and momentum. Stop waiting to feel ready and start acting like your story matters.

Because it does.

> *Most people underestimate what they can achieve in five years because they set goals based on comfort, not calling. Playing small doesn't protect you. It just makes the gap between where you are and where you could be more expensive to close.*

Course Correction Reflections

Q1

Where have you been playing small in your financial life, and what has it actually cost you in dollars, not just confidence?

Q2

What would you charge, ask for, or pursue if you priced yourself at your actual value instead of what feels safe?

CHAPTER THREE

The Mindset That Money Respects

> *Money doesn't respond to hustle. It responds to alignment.*

We've all said some kind of variation of this: "If I could just get the money I need, I'd be all set." But remember, most of us don't have a money problem—we have a *mindset* problem. Money doesn't chase titles, good intentions, or people stuck in survival mode. It moves where it feels respected. It flows to people who are prepared to make room for it and grow it. It's not the hustle you're lacking. It's a shift in how you see money and, more importantly, how you see yourself in relation to it.

Money Isn't the Goal. It's the Tool.

So many of us tie our identity to money. If we have it, we're winning, and if we don't, we're behind. But money was meant to serve you, not define you. It's not a measure of worth. It's a resource like water, time, or energy, and just like those other resources, it needs direction and intention; otherwise, it evaporates. If your mindset hasn't caught up with your vision, you'll burn through every check trying to prove you've made it instead of building something that lasts.

We all know how to spend money, but not enough of us know how to *use* it. We spend it to feel better, to catch up, and to prove to others that we're doing all right. But money isn't meant to be proof of anything. It's meant to be planted, for everything that you're growing that's on its way to you. Money is a seed, and if you want it to grow, you have to plant it in the right soil, water it consistently, and give it time. That's thinking like a *builder*, not a buyer.

And as fun as it may seem at the time, spending to feel better or to catch up or to prove your worth to everyone else aren't character flaws. They're those survival decisions we mentioned earlier. When emotional relief, social belonging, and a sense of normalcy have all been funded by spending, that pattern doesn't disappear just because your income changes. It runs on automatic until something interrupts it. That interruption is what this chapter is about: recognizing the survival decision in the moment before you make it, and asking whether it's still serving you or whether it's just familiar.

You Don't Have to Be Wealthy to Think Wealthy

Some people were born into wealth, and others were born into wisdom. Some were born into both. But if you weren't born into either, you'll have to *choose* to grow into them. But the great part is that you don't need a six-figure income to act like someone who builds wealth—you just need to start asking yourself better questions:

What can I do with what I already have?

How can I stop leaking money into things that don't allow my growth?

Who can I align with who sees value in what I bring?

Things become so much easier when you realize this mindset, because it's the bridge between where you are and the life you want.

Money Moves Through Alignment

Money responds to structure, not stress. It respects people who treat it well, use it wisely, and don't worship it. And instead of chasing it, you just need to build the kind of life that it can flow into. How? By building clarity, systems, and a purpose that amounts to more than just paying bills. When money knows where it's going, it shows up more often (and it stays longer, too).

It's about being prepared, not perfect. Because once you shift your mindset, you'll stop chasing money altogether and start walking in alignment with where it's already trying to go.

Earning more won't fix poor money habits. In most cases, it'll just magnify them. Without the right mindset and structure, money rarely stays where it lands. Building wealth starts long before wealth itself shows up. It begins in your decisions and the habits behind them.

Course Correction Reflections

Q1

What can I do with what I already have?

Q2

How can I stop leaking money into things that don't push me forward?

CHAPTER FOUR

Fear Isn't a Strategy

> *Fear might keep you safe, but it'll never make you wealthy.*

Fear is persuasive, and it wears a lot of disguises. It's dressed up in all the false reassurances we tell ourselves:

I'm just being realistic.

I need more time.

This doesn't feel safe.

Underneath all those comfort statements? Still fear. And left unchecked, you'll keep pretending you're safe while ultimately postponing your purpose. You can't move toward wealth and worship fear at the same time. Remember that fear isn't a strategy. It never was, and it never will be.

Fear Feels Real, But It's a Liar

The hesitation you feel before hitting send. The panic that consumes you after checking your bank account. The doubt that creeps in when opportunity knocks. Fear isn't always loud. Sometimes it whispers, "I'm not ready," "I've never seen anyone like me do this before," or "I don't want to fail." But fear doesn't do anything except make you wait. And waiting doesn't build wealth.

Most people abandon their dreams not because they're lazy, but because they're scared to be seen, scared to want more and not get it. But you can't outwork what you're too afraid to face. Fear lingers in procrastination, people-pleasing, and perfectionism. Until you confront it, it'll remain in control of you.

Fear Is Contagious, But So Is Courage

Your circle matters. If you surround yourself with people who live in fear, you'll start shrinking your goals to match theirs. But bravery is infectious, too, and that's why environment is everything. Choose people, places, and practices that remind you who you are, not who you're afraid to become. Whether it's through prayer, therapy, or mentorship, you need to build systems that keep you rooted in clarity, not fear.

Let Fear Stretch You, Not Stop You

To be completely fair, not all fear is bad. Sometimes it shows up when you're about to grow: the tightness before a leap, the hesitation before a decision, the pause before something shifts. Let that fear motivate you to prepare, not procrastinate. Allow it to sharpen your focus, not shrink your reach. Don't worry about being completely fearless in the things you approach. You just need to move through fear with intention.

You were built with power and equipped with vision. Growth is part of your design. The voice telling you that you're too late or too inexperienced is fear talking, and it only gains authority when you choose to believe it.

> *Most people do have enough talent to move themselves forward, but what holds them back is allowing their fear to control the timing. It feels safe in the moment, but over time it quietly costs them opportunities they may never get back.*

Course Correction Reflections

Q1

Where is fear currently showing up in your life regarding a financial decision?

Q2

What's one move you've been putting off that courage would unlock?

CHAPTER FIVE

Wealth Starts with Identity

> *If your identity is fractured, your wealth will always feel like it's slipping through your hands.*

Wealth goes far beyond income or appearances. A high salary and an expensive car can look impressive, but neither creates something lasting. Real wealth begins much deeper than a bank account. It starts with how you see yourself.

Wealth Isn't What You Wear. It's What You Carry.

Some of the wealthiest people I know don't wear labels. They wear clarity, and they lead with it. Meanwhile, others with all the things are quietly drowning. Why? Because wealth doesn't come down to the stuff. It comes down to the self. It's your self-worth. Your vision. Your discipline. Your boundaries. You can't buy your way into a solid, clear identity, and the hustle definitely can't build one for you.

Everything grows from how you see yourself. When your identity isn't rooted, you chase validation and spend to feel valuable. It's performative. But when your identity feels grounded, your decisions begin to change. You ask better questions and move with more intention. The way you build starts to reflect what matters to you. Success stops feeling like a finish line and starts looking more like a reflection of what you believe you deserve.

Internal Poverty Will Sabotage External Wealth

You can't out-earn a broken identity, nor can you build lasting wealth from shame, fear, or the need to prove something. Wealth is internal first, and it's grounded in peace, purpose, clarity, and conviction. Without those attributes, you'll keep chasing but never feel secure. With them, you'll build from overflow, not obligation.

You may not have been able to choose your starting point, but you do get to choose your direction, and that choice comes from how you define yourself. It shouldn't come from debt or from the weight of old expectations, but from truth. You were created with capacity and built to grow. Your wealth isn't something waiting for you in the future. It exists now.

Your Story Isn't Finished

If you've made it this far into the book, you've already outgrown an older version of yourself. That's part of growth. The people who build lasting wealth aren't focused on proving they've changed; instead, they live in a way that makes change visible. Your value can be easy to lose sight of, especially after years of doubt or delay. This chapter has been a reminder of what was always there, and the rest of this book will keep building on that.

You're not too late to become who you were meant to be. Wealth is built by people who know who they are and who act from that place. The next level starts within you. That's where everything else has to be built from.

Course Correction Reflections

Q1

How do you currently see yourself in relation to wealth, and is that view serving you?

Q2

What identity shift, made right now, would most change your financial reality?

BONUS SECTION

Wealth Identity Reset

> *If you don't know who's running the show, you'll keep repeating the same story with different numbers.*

Before you can build wealth, you need to understand the decision making system that's been running your finances, almost certainly without you fully realizing it.

Remember: Every financial decision you make is either a survival decision or a wealth decision. Survival decisions protect what you have. Wealth decisions build what you don't have yet. Both have their place. The problem is that survival decisions often continue long after the conditions that created them have changed. Money tends to reflect mindset, and mindset is shaped by the identity currently in charge.

The four wealth identities below are a practical map for understanding how your financial decisions are shaped. They show where your financial decisions are coming from right now and where change needs to happen. They show you where your financial decision making is calibrated right now, and also where it needs to go.

The Four Wealth Identities

Circle the identity below that best describes how you currently see money, and underline the identity you're growing into.

The Survivor sees money as safety. Every decision is reactive: pay the bills, keep the lights on, and hope nothing unexpected happens. Your strength is resilience because you know how to stretch. Your risk is confusing surviving with stability.

The Striver sees money as a measure of effort. You're hustling and working harder than most, but wealth still feels out of reach. Your strength is drive because you don't quit. Your risk is exhaustion because you confuse busyness with progress.

The Builder sees money as structure. You've started budgeting, saving, and maybe even investing. You're learning to put systems in place instead of relying on hustle alone. Your strength is strategy because you're playing the long game. Your risk is hesitation—getting stuck over-planning instead of activating.

The Legacy-Maker sees money as alignment. You're no longer just building for yourself; you're building for what lasts. Your strength is clarity because your money has direction. Your risk is complacency, forgetting that every season requires fresh intention.

Where Are You Now?

Today, I most identify as:

____

I'm committed to growing into:

____

Action Step: One Shift Forward

Survivor → Striver: Take one small, intentional step beyond survival. Set aside $10, or learn one new financial concept this week.

Striver → Builder: Create a system (e.g., a budget, an automation, or a debt plan) instead of just more hustle.

Builder → Legacy-Maker: Focus on impact. Teach something, give with structure, or create one system that'll outlast your daily involvement.

You don't graduate from these identities overnight, and you can't skip steps, because each one prepares you for the next. Wealth is a process of growth and constant adjustment. Reset your identity, and keep building from there.

The Shift: From Elevate to Leverage

You've done the work to elevate your mindset. You've challenged old beliefs and started to reclaim the identity that lasting wealth requires. That alone is a victory—because without a new mindset, no amount of strategy will matter. But mindset alone won't build wealth. A renewed perspective is like clearing the fog on the windshield. You can finally see where you're going. But to move forward, it's essential to put the car into gear. That's where leverage comes into play, because it activates the value that's already in you. Mindset says, "I'm capable." And leverage proves it.

PART II

LEVERAGE What You Know

Turn Skills, Lived Experience & Knowledge Into Financial Momentum

CHAPTER SIX

Your Skills Are Already Valuable

> *You don't need to become someone else to earn more. You just need to see the value in who you already are.*

Many people spend years believing they need another degree or more experience before they can start building wealth. In most cases, that delay has very little to do with ability. The value is already there. What matters is recognizing it and putting it to work.

Leverage means turning what you already know into income, opportunity, and freedom. When you start seeing your skills and your lived experience as assets—not just background—you unlock real earning power. But first, you have to stop downplaying your genius.

Why You've Been Undervaluing Yourself

Were you taught that only hard work is worthwhile? That humility means not talking about what you're good at? That your skills aren't worth anything unless someone else confirms it? If so, it makes sense that you've been minimizing your magic. But your lived experience is equity. Your voice, your perspective, and your clarity have value. They can shape real opportunities when you know how to use them. The people who profit from their skills are often the ones who recognize what they have, and move with intention and strategy.

What comes easy to you might be invaluable to someone else. The things people always come to you for, the problems you solve without even thinking, and the experiences you've moved through that others are still navigating—all those things are your leverage. You don't need something new, you just need a clearer way of seeing what's already there.

Skill Doesn't Always Mean Labor

Most of us were taught to trade time for money, and that model creates hard limits. When income depends entirely on your hours, growth becomes difficult to sustain. What if your words earned money while you slept? What if your story became a system? What if your expertise powered a product that didn't require you to show up every time someone needed it? That's leverage. And it's not reserved for people with large platforms or professional credentials. It's available to anyone willing to stop seeing their knowledge as ordinary.

> *Research consistently shows that professionals who reframe their expertise as transferable assets earn significantly more than equally skilled peers who don't. Shift your focus away from selling hours. Build around what you know and how that knowledge can keep creating value. In other words, stop selling labor, and start packaging knowledge.*

Course Correction Reflections

Q1

What skills, knowledge, or experiences do you have that others regularly ask you about?

Q2

What would it look like to turn one of those things into income, even just a small amount?

CHAPTER SEVEN

The Money's in the Overlooked Zones

> *The income you're looking for is often hiding in the areas you've been trained to ignore.*

Most people look for income in the same places: a raise, a second job, or a side hustle that everyone else is already doing. But real leverage lives in the gaps, in the overlooked spaces between what the market offers and what people actually need. You've been taught to look for opportunity where it's obvious: degrees, titles, 9-to-5 promotions, and safe industries. But wealth often hides in the overlooked zones, the places within your skillset and community that don't necessarily show up on a resume but *do* carry real market value.

The question isn't whether you have value; of course you do. It's whether you're seeing all of it. The money isn't always where the crowds are. In fact, sometimes it's where nobody's paying attention. You don't need to force your way into saturated spaces to succeed, but you do need to pause and ask, *What do I do that others avoid or overlook? What strengths do I take for granted because they come easy? What do I know that others need but can't Google?*

That's often where the strongest opportunities begin: in the things that feel ordinary to you, but solve a real problem for someone else.

Your Story Points to the Zone

Your lived experience—especially the hard parts—often points directly to an overlooked market. What have you navigated that others are still figuring out? What system, process, or approach did you have to build from scratch because nothing existed for you? That gap is a business, and make no mistake: it's also leverage.

Think about where your skills and an unmet need intersect. That intersection is often where the most durable and profitable work takes shape. You don't need to be the best in the world; you just need to be clearly useful to the right person with the right problem. Life experience that others are just starting to navigate—soft skills like communication and resilience, systems you created to survive, cultural fluency, trust within a niche community—these are overlooked zones. And what you've been taught to downplay might be the exact thing that opens the next door for you.

> *Sometimes wealth is subtle, not boisterously loud. But if you stop dismissing what comes easy, you'll stop missing what pays well.*

Course Correction Reflections

Q1

What do I do naturally that others always ask me about or thank me for?

Q2

What's one overlooked zone in my life I could start extracting value from this month?

CHAPTER EIGHT

Multiple Streams Don't Mean Multiple Hustles

> *You weren't built to burn out. You were built to build systems that multiply.*

So many of us have been taught that getting ahead means juggling constant work, multiple jobs, and endless side hustles. That mindset creates exhaustion long before it creates wealth. Multiple streams of income should come from deliberate structure, with income built in layers that support each other instead of draining you.

Hustle culture glorifies struggle. It tells you that sleepless nights and working five times harder than everyone else is the only path to wealth. But if the hustle doesn't lead to ownership, it's just expensive labor. Real wealth comes from alignment: aligned work, aligned value, and aligned systems. More streams should bring more freedom, not more fatigue.

Start With One Strong Anchor

Don't start with seven ideas. Start with one. Build one strong offer, then stack new streams around it. Your core offer is the anchor, from which your other streams are branches. When everything aligns with a central skillset, audience, or mission, you multiply impact without multiplying burnout. The goal here is to layer. One audience with multiple entry points, one core skill with different applications, and one brand with several aligned offers.

Streams should flow with or without you, which means digital products, affiliate partnerships, licensing, programs, or offers you can delegate or automate. Ownership means designing income that works, even when you don't. This is how real entrepreneurs build empires. Think of it as though you're building an ecosystem, because you are.

> *Multiple streams should multiply peace, not problems. Start where you are. Stack with purpose, and scale with intention.*

Course Correction Reflections

Q1

What's your current primary income source, and is it strong enough to build from?

Q2

What's one system, product, or offer you could build that would generate income without requiring your constant presence?

CHAPTER NINE

Price Your Power

> *Stop charging based on what you think they can afford. Start charging based on what it's worth for them to walk away with your brilliance.*

It's hard to build real wealth when you're constantly undercharging, overexplaining, or apologizing for your rates. Many talented people stay financially stuck because they've been trained to undervalue what they bring to the table. The skill is there; the problem is often the habit of treating that skill as smaller than it is.

Have you ever thought to yourself, *I don't want to seem greedy, What if they say no?*, or *This doesn't feel like enough work to justify charging that amount*? That approach comes from scarcity and shame, even when it might seem like humility. You're not asking for too much—you're *over-explaining.* Most of the time, you're charging based on what you think the client can afford, or what someone else in your circle charges, or your own insecurities rather than your solution's actual value.

Charge for the Outcome, Not the Hours

The most powerful shift in wealth-building is to stop pricing by time. Instead, start pricing by transformation. What's it worth for someone to gain clarity, confidence, or results faster? What's the value for them to become unstuck? What would they pay someone else to solve this problem inefficiently? You're saving people time, stress, and trial-and-error. That makes your work an investment, not an expense.

Trying to be affordable for everyone is the fastest way to burn out, attract the wrong audience, build resentment toward your own work, and remain in a state of lack. There's nothing noble or affordable about being accessible but exhausted. Wealth is built when your pricing respects your boundaries, your energy, and your expertise. Say your price with conviction, and believe it. Confidence closes more deals than discounts ever will.

> *Research consistently shows that women underprice their services compared to equally or more qualified men—and men themselves often fall victim to the same scarcity mindset. Stop shrinking the price to match the client's comfort. You need to elevate the price to match your value.*

Course Correction Reflections

Q1

In what areas have you felt unsure about how to price your skills or services?

Q2

What would it look like to price in alignment with your experience and the results you create?

CHAPTER TEN

Position, Don't Chase

> *The right opportunities don't need to be chased, only recognized and received.*

Once you've acknowledged your skills and started charging with confidence, there's one more shift that completes your leverage play: you must position yourself. Because being talented, certified, or "helpful" isn't enough. It's about more than just doing the work—you need to be *seen* doing it.

Why Positioning Matters More Than Hustling

When you're positioned properly, people come to you. Your price feels justified, and you're trusted even before you pitch. You repel timewasters and attract serious clients, partners, or investors. But when you're chasing, you second-guess yourself, negotiate your worth, and burn out doing the most for the least. Positioning is leverage. It says, *I know my lane, and I know what I bring to it.*

The truth is that most of us only have ourselves to blame for remaining invisible because of fear of judgment, imposter syndrome, not wanting to outshine others, or worrying about not being ready yet. But we grow by showing up, not by hiding. If people don't know what you do, how you do it, and why it matters, they can't pay you, refer you, or respect you. Visibility is part of the strategy. If people can't see your work, they have no reason to trust it or pay for it.

Positioning Doesn't Equal Performing

Positioning comes from making sure how you present yourself matches the value you actually provide. Ask yourself: *What do I want to be known for? Where does my credibility already live? Who do I serve best, and how can they find me?* Now show up there boldly with intention and consistency. Despite what social media might tell you, you don't need a viral moment. You need a clear voice in the right space.

Stop spending your energy on clients who don't value your work, because time spent chasing the wrong opportunities usually leads to more frustration, not more growth. Strong careers are built through the right partnerships, fair compensation, and a reputation that keeps working for you even when you're not in the room. You rise by standing tall and letting the right things meet you where you are.

> *Professionals known for one clear area of expertise consistently earn more than equally skilled generalists. Clear positioning leads to better opportunities, and clarity makes it easier for people to say yes.*

The Shift: From Leverage to Invest

You've learned how to leverage your background, skills, and positioning. You've taken what felt ordinary and discovered how it holds extraordinary value. But leverage without direction can only take you so far. You can position, package, and price your value, but if you don't multiply it, you'll stay stuck in the same cycle of work. That's where invest comes in. Leverage asks, *What do you already have? Invest asks, What will you grow?*

PART III

INVEST with Intention

Demystifying the Money Moves That Create Long-Term Wealth

CHAPTER ELEVEN

Understand the Game Before You Play It

> *You don't have to be rich to start investing, but you do have to stop living like wealth is accidental.*

It's a fair assumption that plenty of us treat investing as something reserved for the wealthy, when in reality it's one of the main ways wealth gets built. But too many people stay on the sidelines, either because they're intimidated, uninformed, or convinced that it's not for them. This chapter focuses on understanding how the game works and why money moves the way it does. The tools may change, but the principles behind them matter first.

Wealth Is *Not* Income

Income is what you earn. Wealth is what you keep, grow, and pass on. You can make six figures and still be broke, and you can also have a modest salary and still build long-term wealth. Why? Because wealth isn't measured by how fast the money comes in—it's measured by how smart it moves when it does. The true goal is *ownership*: assets that grow in value, money that earns while you sleep, and something that lasts longer than your next paycheck. These are wealth questions, and they start with understanding that every dollar has a job, and some jobs pay you back over and over again.

Know the Players, Know the Rules

You wouldn't join a sport without knowing how the points are scored, so why play the money game blindly? Start with the basics:

An asset puts money in your pocket; a liability takes money out.

The wealthy accumulate assets; the financially stuck often accumulate liabilities.

Cash flow is the money moving in and out monthly; net worth is what you own minus what you owe.

All these things are within your control. Equity is ownership stake, in a home, a business, or an investment. Debt is obligation, and strategic use of debt to build equity is how most generational wealth begins.

Then go deeper. What's your risk tolerance? Conservative investors prioritize stability, while aggressive investors chase growth. Neither is wrong, but knowing yourself keeps you from panicking when markets move. What are your short- and long-term goals? The investments that make sense at 25 are different from those at 45. Are you building income, wealth, or both? The more you understand the language of money, the more confident you become in using it as a tool, not something that entraps you.

Why Knowing Isn't Enough

What many financial books avoid saying honestly or plainly is that people rarely stay on the investment sidelines because they lack information. More often, the gap is between knowing what to do and being able to act on it. You can understand that investing builds wealth, nod along to the difference between assets and liabilities, and read every chapter of this book—and still open zero investment accounts. This is because the part of you that makes the actual decision (the one that pauses when you're about to move money somewhere unfamiliar) is still making a survival decision: *Keep what you have. Don't risk it. You might need it.* That's your nervous system doing exactly what it was built to do, approaching things from a scarcity mindset.

The shift from *knowing* to *doing* requires recognizing the survival decision in the moment it happens and naming it for what it is: a habit. When you feel the resistance before opening an investment account, automating a transfer, or moving money somewhere you can't immediately see and touch, that feeling has a name now. It's a survival decision asking for permission to run the show one more time. You need to be able to see it clearly enough to choose something different.

Beware the Hustle Loop

Make money, spend it all, hustle again, repeat. This is the cycle that most of us fall victim to, but investing is how you exit the loop. It might mean a retirement account you contribute to monthly, a business that earns while you sleep, or real estate that appreciates while you're on vacation. It starts small, but it starts now. But before you put money into any asset, ask yourself this: *Have I invested in myself?* Your mindset is an asset. Your skillset is an asset. Your confidence, clarity, and consistency? All assets. You are your first portfolio.

The average person with lasting wealth has multiple income streams, and most started with just one. Stop waiting to be rich to build wealth. Start learning now, and wealth will follow.

Course Correction Reflections

Q1

What have you believed about investing that no longer serves you?

Q2

What would it mean to see yourself as someone who builds wealth on purpose?

CHAPTER TWELVE

Stop Saving, Start Owning

> *Saving protects. Investing multiplies. You need both.*

If you were raised like most people out there, saving was the holy grail of financial wisdom. *Put something aside for a rainy day. Don't touch your savings. As long as you've got something saved, you're okay.* That said, no one is denying that saving absolutely matters. It's smart, protective, creates options. But you can't save your way to wealth, and that's the part that most financial advice skips over. Saving is a survival decision at its best. It protects what you have, keeps danger at bay, and gives you something solid to stand on. There's nothing wrong with it—until it becomes the only move you make.

Here's why. If you save $10,000 in a basic savings account earning 0.01% interest, you'll have $10,001 after one year. Meanwhile, inflation quietly grows 3% to 6% per year. Your money may look safe, but it's losing buying power. Saving equals protection, and investing equals growth. You need both, but don't confuse them.

Why We Default to Saving

There's a reason saving feels easier. It's predictable because you can see the number. It's what we were taught, especially if we didn't grow up with role models when it came to investing. And it just feels safer; we've all seen people lose their money and thought, *Well, that'll never be me.* But safe doesn't always mean optimal, and familiar doesn't necessarily mean financially free. You were taught to save for emergencies, but who taught you to invest for expansion?

This isn't a knock on saving but rather a reframe of its role. Savings should fund your emergency cushion (three to six months of expenses), your short-term goals (a vacation, a car, a home down payment), and your transition periods when life pivots unexpectedly. But if saving is your only move, you're working against time instead of with it. Owning means building equity instead of just tucking money away. It means that your dollars are growing while you sleep, setting you up for freedom rather than just security. Saving helps you survive, but investing helps you scale.

> *Over a 10-year period, the average savings account grows at well under 1%, while even conservative investments can grow significantly faster. Saving keeps you afloat, while investing moves you forward.*

Course Correction Reflections

Q1

What role has saving played in your financial life, and has it been enough?

Q2

What's one step you could take in the next 30 days toward owning something?

CHAPTER THIRTEEN

Let Your Money Move

> *Every dollar is an employee. If it's not working for you, it's working for someone else.*

Money is often treated like the final goal, but it's actually the tool. It is meant to be used with purpose, not left sitting still. Left untouched, savings lose value over time, but put to work wisely, they have the chance to build something larger.

Here's what stagnant money looks like: saving without strategy, spending without clarity, investing without intention, and earning without direction. Unassigned money always finds somewhere to go, and it's usually toward emotional spending, lifestyle creep, or fear-based hoarding. The problem is rarely the money itself, and more often the lack of movement and direction behind it. Wealth grows when money is handled with intention and kept in motion. That kind of flow creates freedom.

Automate with Intention

The wealthy don't manage every dollar one by one or by hand. They set systems:

Auto-transferring money into a high-yield savings account.

Setting recurring contributions to their investment accounts.

Using micro-investment tools to put spare change to work.

Build a system that grows your net worth while you sleep. The goal is to remove friction so that your money keeps working without needing constant attention.

Ask yourself: Is this money just *sitting* with me, or is it *working* with me? Does this dollar have a job, or is it just waiting to be used? And the question that changes everything: If I stopped working tomorrow, would any part of my income continue to flow? That last one is worth spending some time with for a while.

> *Studies consistently show that people who automate their investments stay more consistent, and build more wealth over time. Allow your money to move, and then allow your life to expand.*

Course Correction Reflections

Q1

Where is your money just sitting with you instead of working with you?

Q2

What's one simple step you can take this week to put your money into motion?

CHAPTER FOURTEEN

Grow What You Understand

> *You don't need to master every market. You need to master your moves.*

Between crypto headlines, real estate gurus, and social media finance trends, it's easy to feel like you're already behind. It's as though if you're not investing in 12 things, you've missed the moment. But wealth is built on understanding, not impulse. You don't need to chase every trend. You need a clear approach that fits your life and your decisions.

When you chase what's hot, you feel scattered instead of strategic. You can't explain what you own or why. You're driven by headlines and buzzwords and trends, not goals. You hesitate instead of act. Most wealth is built in repeatable systems, which involves knowing how the investment earns, being aware of the risk, and having a strategy rather than just a feeling. Confident investors stick with the plan longer. That's how they grow.

Start with What Aligns

What kind of investing feels natural or interesting to you? What asset class aligns with your strengths or learning style? Who do you trust to teach it in a way that you truly get? If you love research, look into stocks, ETFs, and index funds. If tangible assets interest you, consider real estate and property. If you're into ideas and innovation, explore business ownership, brands, and intellectual property. Start where you understand, then go deeper.

A focused portfolio of two or three well-understood assets is so much more effective than a scattered mess of trendy guesses. Complexity can look impressive, but clarity actually compounds. Stay with the process. Learn it well. And then allow it to grow.

> *Investors who consistently use one or two strategies they understand tend to significantly outperform trend-chasers over time. Clarity beats chaos, each and every time.*

Course Correction Reflections

Q1

In what areas are you investing from a place of pressure and not clarity?

Q2

What's one investment vehicle you could commit to learning deeply before adding anything else?

CHAPTER FIFTEEN

Don't Just Accumulate. Activate.

> *Wealth isn't what you have. It's what you do with what you have.*

By this point in the book, you've learned how to shift your mindset, own your value, and invest with purpose. But there's one more trap that silently stalls progress, even when everything looks right on paper. You begin to accumulate savings, assets, or opportunity, and then you stop moving. You wait. You hesitate. You hold back, hoping that the perfect move will reveal itself. But wealth grows when what you have is put to work. Possession alone is never enough.

It's easy to mistake accumulation for progress: stacking cash but never deploying it, collecting knowledge but avoiding applying it, and owning assets you never optimize or leverage. But unactuated wealth is just stored potential, and stored potential isn't freedom. Activation looks like turning a savings cushion into seed capital, leveraging real estate for strategic growth, using business profits to invest in people or systems, and monetizing your knowledge to create income-producing assets.

This is about being ready to use what you've built. You've earned the right to move with confidence.

Wealth Is a Cycle, Not a Shelf

True wealth comes from using what you have well, and it grows through movement and the willingness to reinvest. The most powerful wealth builders activate, evaluate, and repeat. The real question is how well you're using what you already have. Wealth grows through movement and deliberate use, and legacy is built through action.

> *Many people with savings, assets, or business income admit that they don't use it to grow anything because they're afraid to mess up. Money grows when it's used with purpose and kept in motion.*

The Shift: From Investing to Being Tidy

You've learned the power of investing, but the key thing to remember is that growth without order quickly collapses. You can grow your income and build more opportunity, but if your systems are messy and your habits are inconsistent, money slips away as quickly as it arrives. Being tidy is all about protection, not restricting yourself. Investing asks, *Where will your money multiply?* Being tidy asks, *How will you protect and direct it?*

PART IV

Tidy & Tune Your Finances

You Can't Elevate What's Out of Order.

Build Systems That Give You Peace and Power.

CHAPTER SIXTEEN

Tidy Up to Build Up

> *Messy money makes slow progress.*

You can't grow what you're avoiding. You can't manage what you can't see. And you definitely can't build something solid on a foundation of chaos. Disorganization drains energy and creates unnecessary friction. Financial chaos usually means your systems need attention and a better structure, not that you've been failing. You just need a mindset shift.

When your money is messy, you start avoiding your accounts, missing due dates, feeling shame or stress when you spend, and starting systems you never stick with. Eventually you hear yourself saying things like, *I'll figure it out later. I'll fix it as soon as I start making more. It's too overwhelming right now.* But remember, more money doesn't fix a messy system. Clarity comes first, and then growth follows.

Financial chaos is generally the result of years spent managing money in survival mode. It looks like paying the most urgent bill first and avoiding the accounts that create anxiety, or spending for a moment of relief from constant financial pressure. Those patterns are the result of a system trained to respond that way. The shift from chaos to clarity is the transition away from managing crisis and toward managing wealth. And it starts with being willing to look.

The Two-Part Reset: Tidy + Tune

Tidying means visibility. Gather all accounts, bills, debts, subscriptions, assets, and income sources in one place. Make a list, use a spreadsheet, pull up your apps… Whatever works, but just get it all out of your head and into a place where you can see it.

Tuning means alignment. Assign a purpose to each account. Set clear financial goals, and eliminate cluttered tools or duplicated systems. Create a money rhythm, whether it's weekly, biweekly, or monthly.

Tidying gives you control, and tuning gives you direction.

When you know your numbers—even if they're not where you want them to be, you reclaim your power. Messy money is rarely just about dollars. It carries emotional weight, and that weight shapes how decisions are made. When you clean it up, that weight lifts. Pick your money day, and use it to review balances, update your budget, track upcoming bills and income. Also use it to shift money where it needs to go, and reflect on spending and progress. Wealthy people don't wing it. They review, adjust, and reallocate—and they do it proactively.

> *Those who track their finances regularly are far more likely to reach their goals and report significantly less financial stress. Discipline creates freedom. It gives your money direction instead of leaving every decision to stress or impulse.*

Course Correction Reflections

Q1

What part of your finances feels the most disorganized or unclear right now?

Q2

What would financial clarity look and feel like at this point in your life?

CHAPTER SEVENTEEN

Make Your Money Manageable

> *If your money system doesn't fit your real life, it won't survive your next season.*

You've probably tried the budget binder that gathered dust, the spreadsheet you updated once and then forgot about, the app that felt like homework, or the viral method that didn't match your lifestyle. But all your money needs is a rhythm that respects your reality, not the "perfect" plan.

Most budgeting systems fail because they're too strict to maintain, too vague to be useful, and too disconnected from real life. They're often rooted in shame instead of strategy, and control instead of clarity. A solid money system supports you, not punishes or overwhelms you.

Forget Budgeting. Focus on Flow.

Instead of obsessing over every line item, ask yourself three questions:

What's coming in?

What's going out?

Is it flowing in a way that reflects my goals?

That's it. Flow-based money management builds awareness without shame and encourages consistency over control. You don't need to track every penny. You just need to know where your energy is going.

All you need is clarity in three core areas:

- Your income streams (how much you make and where it comes from)
- Your fixed versus flexible expenses (fixed things like rent, insurance, and subscriptions vs. flexible things like groceries, gas, and lifestyle spending)
- Your intentional allocations, or where you direct your money with purpose (savings, debt payoff, investments, giving, reinvestment, etc.)

Start simple, then grow when you're ready. Wealth is built through steady momentum. Small actions repeated consistently do far more than constant micromanagement.

> *People who use a simple but consistent money system are significantly more likely to avoid consumer debt, as well as more likely to invest. Complexity looks smart, but consistency builds wealth.*

Course Correction Reflections

Q1

What's one financial habit that's never worked for me, and why?

Q2

What would a supportive money system look like at this point in my life?

CHAPTER EIGHTEEN

Automate the Discipline

> *Discipline is easier when it's built into the system, not forced by willpower.*

Remember, most people struggle with money for two reasons: because life is overwhelming and because willpower runs thin. We're managing work, family, deadlines, and decisions, and even the best intentions can fall apart when we rely on constant effort. That's where automation comes in. The goal is to build a system that keeps moving forward, even on the days when your energy is low.

Willpower is a limited resource. You can only make so many decisions in a day before decision fatigue sets in. That's why the best financial habit is often the one that doesn't require any decision at all. When your savings, investments, and bill payments happen automatically, you remove the single biggest barrier to financial discipline: the moment of choice.

What to Automate First

Start with four things:

- **Savings:** Set up an automatic transfer to a dedicated savings or emergency fund account on payday, before you can spend it.
- **Investments:** Set up recurring contributions to your retirement account, index fund, or investment app of choice.
- **Bills:** Automate fixed monthly expenses so that you never miss a due date or pay a late fee again.
- **Philanthropy:** If generosity is a core value, automate a small recurring gift to a cause that matters to you.

Automate the things that align with your goals and spend consciously on everything else.

Automation works best when it's set with intention and reviewed regularly. Once a month, check your automations: *Are amounts still appropriate for this season? Is anything overdrawn or misaligned? Is there a new goal I should be funding?* Automation removes friction, and frequent reviews keep it aligned with your life. What you're working toward is a financial life that runs well, even on your worst days.

> *Research has repeatedly shown that people who automate their financial habits stay more consistent and build more wealth over time. When you remove the decision, you protect the result.*

Course Correction Reflections

Q1

What financial task do you consistently put off that you could automate?

____

____

____

____

____

____

Q2

What would it feel like to have your savings and investments happening automatically, without giving them a second thought?

____

____

____

____

____

____

CHAPTER NINETEEN

Kill the "I'll Just Catch Up" Lie

> *There's no catching up. There's only starting <u>now.</u>*

Does any of this sound familiar?

I'll get serious about money when I make more of it.

I'll start saving when the kids are older.

I'll invest once I pay off this debt.

These are the lies you've likely been telling yourself, and every single one of them is costing you money you'll never get back.

"Later" sounds responsible; it sounds like you're waiting until you're ready. But financially speaking, "later" is one of the most expensive decisions you can make. The math is brutal: Every year you delay investing, you lose the compounding growth that would've been working for you. A $200/month investment started at age 25 can grow into far more than the same investment at 35, even if the person starting later ends up contributing more overall. Time is the one investment advantage you can never buy back.

The reasons we wait feel valid. *I don't have enough to make a difference. I need to fix my spending first. I don't know enough yet.* But beginning with small amounts now will always outperform beginning with large amounts later. Progress starts with a pulse and a starting line. It begins when you decide to act, even in a small way. Ten dollars a month matters more than waiting for the perfect amount. A small transfer into savings creates a habit, and that habit changes how you think about money. Compounding begins the moment you start. The choice is whether that begins today or later.

What matters about "later" is that it usually has very little to do with time. More often, it's a survival decision that feels safer when framed as planning. When you're operating in survival mode, the future is abstract and the present is urgent. "Later" is how the survival brain manages the gap between what it knows it should do and what feels too risky to do right now. It often looks like procrastination, but underneath, it's usually a form of protection. The way to interrupt that pattern begins with the right question, not more guilt or forced urgency. Next time you hear yourself say, "I'll deal with this later," stop and ask: *Is this a survival decision or a wealth decision?* Because survival decisions feel responsible. They feel like you're being careful. But they have a cost, and that cost compounds the same way interest does—just in the wrong direction.

> *The most powerful variable in building wealth is time. Income matters, and so does knowledge, but time is what allows both to compound. Every day you delay is a day of compounding you cannot reclaim. Start today, with whatever you have.*

Course Correction Reflections

Q1

What financial action have you been delaying, and what has that delay cost you?

Q2

What's one small step you could take today to stop waiting and start building?

CHAPTER TWENTY

Give Every Dollar a Job

> *Unassigned money is money that disappears.*

By this point, you've got a solid command of how to tidy, tune, and automate. Now we bring it all together with one of the most powerful principles in financial management: intentional allocation. Every dollar you earn deserves a direction. It should know where it's going, and why. Restriction is about control, but direction is about purpose. And purposeful money builds wealth, while restricted money builds resentment.

One of the most effective approaches is zero-based thinking: assign every dollar a job until your income, minus your allocations, equals zero. Every dollar should be placed with purpose, whether it's going toward savings, investments, expenses, or giving. When every dollar has a job, nothing wanders into impulse purchases or disappears without explanation.

The Four Jobs Every Dollar Can Have

Think of your money as having four possible assignments:

- **Protect:** emergency fund, insurance, debt payoff
- **Grow:** investments, retirement, education
- **Live:** housing, food, transportation, lifestyle
- **Philanthropy:** tithes, charity, family support (with structure and boundaries)

You choose the percentages and adjust by season. But every dollar needs a clear category before it arrives, not after it's already gone. Write down your monthly take-home income. List every spending category in your lifestyle. Assign a dollar amount to each one, and adjust until every dollar is assigned. Revisit monthly as your lifestyle changes. It doesn't have to be perfect on day one. It needs to reflect your real life and the way you actually make decisions.

> *People who assign their money intentionally—even imperfectly—report less financial stress and more consistent progress toward their goals. A workable plan matters more than waiting for a flawless one. Clear direction is what helps decisions move forward.*

The Shift: From Tidy to Extend

At this point, the foundation is already there, and it's ready to be used in terms of building systems, creating order, and giving your money direction. Your finances are no longer running you—you're running them. The reason that order matters so much is because it creates the foundation everything else depends on, and so the final ELITE principle asks you to look beyond yourself. Tidy asks, *How will you protect and direct your wealth?* Extend asks, *Who else benefits from what you're building?*

PART V

EXTEND the Legacy

Build Wealth That Outlives You

CHAPTER TWENTY-ONE

Define the Win

> *Legacy begins the moment you decide what winning actually means.*

Most people spend their lives chasing success without ever defining what it looks like. They work harder, earn more, and accumulate more, but they still feel like something's missing. That something is often clarity. Not about what's in their account, but about what they're actually building toward and why.

Forget what Instagram says and forget what your cousin with the Tesla tells you. In fact, forget every borrowed idea of what success is "supposed" to look like. What does winning actually look like for you? Not for your parents, your neighborhood, or your social media feed. For *you*. Maybe it's never worrying about a bill again. Maybe it's owning a home free and clear. Maybe it's having real options about how you spend your time, leaving something behind for your children that your parents couldn't leave for you. Or building a business that runs without you. The definition matters. You can't build toward something you haven't named.

From Goals to Legacy

Goals are milestones, and legacy is what the milestones add up to. If you hit every financial goal you've set, what will have changed—not just in your bank account, but in your family, community, and sense of self? That answer is your legacy definition. Write it down. Be specific and make it visual. Share it with someone who'll hold you accountable to it. Your vision is a fragile thing when it's only in your head. Put it somewhere it can be seen and returned to, because life will try to distract you, reduce you, and convince you to settle for less. Your written vision is your resistance.

> *Those of us with a clearly written financial vision are significantly more likely to achieve it than those who keep goals only in their heads. Name the win. Write it down and build toward it deliberately.*

Course Correction Reflections

Q1

In your own words, what does financial "winning" actually look like for you?

Q2

What would you want your wealth to enable for yourself, your family, and beyond?

CHAPTER TWENTY-TWO

Give Without Losing Yourself

> *Generosity is a virtue. But generosity without structure is a trap.*

One of the most common ways that wealth builders get derailed is through giving without limits. You worked hard, built something, and now everyone around you suddenly needs a piece of it. So, you give because you love them, and because it's the right thing to do. Because you remember when you needed help and someone showed up. But somewhere in all that giving, you forget to protect what you built.

The Difference Between Generosity & Sacrifice

Generosity enriches both the giver and the receiver, but sacrifice depletes the giver while the receiver often never builds the capacity to stand on their own. True generosity has structure, a budget, and a limit, and it comes from overflow, not from bleeding your own future dry. In communities where relationships have always been the primary safety net (where your family and your circle are what stand between you and crisis), giving without limits isn't selflessness. It's—you guessed it—another survival decision, one that made complete sense when everyone around you was an emergency away from disaster. The real problem is repeating that same decision after something stronger has started to take shape. Without protecting the foundation, there's nothing left to create the kind of overflow that makes generosity sustainable.

We've all heard the airplane safety instruction, to put your own oxygen mask on before helping others, and the same principle applies here. If you give so much that you deplete your own foundation, you'll eventually have nothing left to give. Protecting your wealth is part of responsible stewardship. It allows what you've built to last and serve a greater purpose.

Budget for giving the same way you budget for bills by making it intentional, not reactive. Separate financial giving from the time and emotional energy you offer. Learning to say no can be an act of love; in some situations, helping someone build for themselves is far more generous than stepping in to build it for them. Decide in advance what you will and won't fund and hold the line. The most sustainable givers build their own foundation first. Protecting your wealth allows your generosity to last. It creates the stability needed to support others now, and to keep that support going for generations.

Course Correction Reflections

Q1

Where have you been giving beyond your means, and what has that cost you?

Q2

What would intentional, structured giving look like in your life?

CHAPTER TWENTY-THREE

Teach What You Know

> *Your wisdom is part of your wealth.*
> *Don't hoard it. Honor it.*

There's someone in your life right this very moment who's currently where *you* were three years ago, struggling with the same fears, carrying the same myths, and making the same financial missteps you've already worked through. And your experience is exactly what they need. When you share what you've learned—the real version, not the polished highlight reel—you give someone else permission to begin. You shorten their learning curve, and you break a cycle. That's legacy in action. It's not just what you leave behind, but also what you multiply while you're still here.

You Don't Need a Title to Teach

Being useful doesn't require a platform, formal credentials, or a lofty job title. What matters is the willingness to be honest about your own journey and clear about what it's taught you. Share how you paid off your first debt. Talk to your kids about how money moves in your household. Mentor a younger colleague about the financial realities of building a career. Have the money conversation with your partner that you've been avoiding. Teaching happens in kitchens, over text messages, across coffee shop tables, and in the kind of honest conversations people remember long after they end.

Wealth Isn't Built Alone

Money touches every relationship you have, whether you talk about it together or not. And if you don't take control of those conversations, money will end up controlling them for you. When you share life with a partner, you share decisions about money. Alignment comes from deliberate choices. It takes intention and consistent attention. In other words, it happens by design. True financial intimacy means being honest about values and priorities, and this is where family can either be your greatest source of support or your greatest source of financial pressure. Legacy is built by modeling discipline and showing others what steadiness looks like over time; it isn't a rescue mission. Your impact grows when you share knowledge and lift as you climb.

> *Mentorship and peer learning dramatically increase financial confidence, especially among first generation wealth builders. Legacy isn't just what you leave behind. It's the conversations you start while you're still here.*

Course Correction Reflections

Q1

What's something you've figured out that others around you are still struggling with?

____

____

____

____

____

____

Q2

Who in your life would benefit most from you sharing your financial journey, and how could you start that conversation?

____

____

____

____

____

____

CHAPTER TWENTY-FOUR

Build Systems That Outlive You

> *Wealth dies in disorganization, but legacy lives in systems.*

You can build real wealth and create meaningful opportunities, but without structure and protection, it can disappear within a generation. It happens frequently—homes are lost, businesses shutter, and accounts get locked. Knowledge disappears with the person who held it. Why? Because the vision was strong, but the systems were missing. If you want your wealth to outlive you, it must be bigger than your presence. It must be built to function *without* you.

What's a Legacy System?

A legacy system is anything that allows your values, guidance, or wealth to keep moving, even when you're no longer around to explain it. It can be a will or a living trust, a business with documented processes, financial accounts with clear beneficiaries, instructions for accessing key assets, or letters and voice notes to future generations. Legacy lasts when it's documented clearly and simplified, enabling it to carry forward.

Too many families are left with the same questions after a loved one passes. Where did they bank? What happens to the house? Who needs to be called first, and what comes next? It's heartbreaking, but it's preventable.

Start documenting now: passwords and logins stored securely; financial contacts, including your CPA and attorney; insurance policies and account numbers; business operating procedures; and your final wishes. Create a digital or physical folder with account information, beneficiaries, legal documents, business assets, and a personal letter outlining your values and intentions. Make it accessible by sharing it with someone you trust. Update it at least once a year. Don't regard any of this as a chore, or as menial paperwork. It protects the people you love, prepares them for difficult moments, and makes your care visible when it matters most.

> *Over 60% of generational wealth is lost by the second generation, and 90% is gone by the third. The number one reason? Lack of structure, documentation, and communication. Build the system now so that your legacy lives later.*

Course Correction Reflections

Q1

What important financial or life information do you hold that no one else knows how to access?

____

____

____

____

____

____

Q2

What's one system or document you could create this month to protect your legacy?

____

____

____

____

____

____

CHAPTER TWENTY-FIVE

The Legacy Is You

> *You're not just building wealth.*
> *You are the wealth.*

Somewhere along the way, this book stopped being about money in theory.

It became an examination about how you live, what you protect, and what your life teaches the people around you. Wealth has never been limited to income or investment accounts. It shows up in your discipline, your decisions, your boundaries, and the standards you refuse to lower.

That leads to the final, and perhaps most important, truth of this book:

The most valuable thing you'll ever pass down is you.

Not only what you earn or what you leave behind, but the example you set while you're here. The way you handle pressure, the consistency that people have come to trust, and the effort people notice even when you think no one is paying attention. That's what teaches. That's what remains.

Every belief you've challenged and every boundary you've learned to protect has shaped more than your own future. It's left a pattern others can follow. People watch how you carry yourself. They learn from what you tolerate, what you walk away from, and what you choose to build. Your legacy is being formed in real time, through the ordinary decisions that quietly teach others what's possible. Even the decision you make to do things differently matters, because it gives someone else permission to begin. When you change your own direction, you also change the starting point for the people around you.

Legacy Is Built While You're Here

There's no finish line, perfect version, or moment where it all clicks and you're done. Legacy is shaped by what you choose each day. It grows through the healing you pursue, the habits you protect, and the way you handle what passes through your hands. It starts with you, and yet it definitely doesn't *end* with you. Your money matters, but your mindset is the foundation. Your structure creates peace, but the story behind it is what gives it power. Keep showing up. Keep refining. Keep extending what you know.

People will never remember every dollar you made. They'll remember how you made decisions, how you showed up, and the patterns you were willing to break.

Wealth is only a tool, but the real change comes through you.

Course Correction Reflections

Q1

What version of you is your family or your future self waiting on right now?

____

____

____

____

____

____

Q2

What mindset, system, or belief have you shifted that could change someone else's life if you shared it?

____

____

____

____

____

____

EPILOGUE

We Carry Forward What They Didn't Teach

> *Some legacies were buried, but others were built loud enough to echo through silence.*

In classrooms across the country, students are taught the names of inventors, politicians, and titans of industry. But you don't often hear the name Maggie Lena Walker.

Born in 1864 to a formerly enslaved mother, Maggie was a schoolteacher who quietly became something far more dangerous to the system: a financial educator and institution builder. She founded the St. Luke Penny Savings Bank, becoming the first woman—of any race—to charter and lead a bank in the United States. And she didn't wait for permission to build her legacy.

In a time when Black families were systemically denied access to fair credit, basic banking, or even reliable pay for their labor, Maggie created a solution that did more than store money. She created a network. Through the Independent Order of St. Luke, she built a platform that combined mutual aid, financial literacy, and economic empowerment. Her bank encouraged families to pool their resources, open accounts in their children's names, and protect what little they had from predatory hands.

What she was doing was teaching others to manage money *themselves*, quietly, powerfully, and intentionally. But she was building institutions while textbooks ignored the work. She was strengthening communities while national financial systems shut them out. She was speaking about ownership and generational responsibility while schools were still teaching obedience instead of agency.

Still, Maggie (and countless women like her) persisted. They passed knowledge hand to hand and built ledgers behind closed doors. They taught principles in kitchens, beauty salons, and prayer circles. This is a buried blueprint with something important to teach. Wealth certainly depends on accumulation, but also on *circulation*. Financial literacy wasn't simply missing from many communities. In many cases, it was deliberately withheld. And this blueprint reminds us that, for many of us, legacy started with a woman who refused to let lack define her power or her community's future.

Maggie Walker built far more than a bank. She created a movement, and that work can continue through the choices you make today.

The Movement Continues

Maggie Walker built her movement with what she had: clarity, conviction, and a deep belief that the people around her deserved better than the system was willing to offer.

That's what this book has been asking of you. Not to expect someone to hand you a blueprint that was never meant for you, but to make the decision to see your story differently, to claim the identity of someone who builds wealth. Not because it was given, but because you chose it—and kept choosing it—one small intentional move at a time. The principles work because *you* do. And now that we're reaching the end of these pages, only one question remains:

What's your next move?

We didn't call this book *Given*. We called it *EARNED*—because that's exactly what it all comes down to.

You earn your independence and legacy through clarity, courage, and the daily decision to build something real on ground that was never designed to hold you. Both are earned by trusting your own hands, your own judgment, and your ability to create something lasting without waiting for permission.

Maggie knew that. Now you do, too.

FINAL REVIEW

The ELITE Framework

Somewhere in these pages, you recognized yourself. Maybe it was in the Survivor: stretching every dollar, managing crisis after crisis, and doing whatever it takes just to hold things together. Survival is real, and the strength it built within you is real. But survival was never meant to be the destination.

Maybe it was in the Striver: working harder than almost everyone around you, hustling across multiple jobs or roles, and believing that if you could just do more, something would finally break through. You have drive that most people will never understand. The shift is learning to work toward something that builds and lasts, instead of pouring energy into what only drains you.

Maybe it was in the Builder: finally putting systems in place, starting to budget with intention, making your first investment, and feeling for the first time like you're playing offense instead of defense. You've started to see that strategy, not just effort, is what creates momentum.

Or maybe you recognized yourself in the Legacy-Maker: thinking beyond yourself; designing wealth that outlives you; and having conversations with your children, your community, your circle that weren't available to you when you needed them most. Wherever you landed, the story keeps moving from there. That's where things start to change.

Let's review our five principles for building lasting wealth one more time:

E—Elevate Your Mindset

Wealth begins within. Unlearn inherited financial beliefs and question the patterns shaped by fear or scarcity. Rebuild your identity as someone capable of creating wealth. Know your worth, trust your story, and move with clear goals.

L—Leverage What You Know

Use your skills and lived experience as real assets. Turn overlooked knowledge into income that fits your life. Price your work with confidence, and position yourself where the right opportunities can find you.

I—Invest with Intention

Money is a tool, and it works best when it has direction. Start where you are and let small decisions build momentum. Use what you understand, and put your assets to work instead of letting them sit untouched.

T—Tidy & Tune Your Finances

Clarity builds confidence. Eliminate financial chaos by creating systems that fit the way you actually live. Make discipline easier through structure, remove unnecessary friction, and give every dollar a clear purpose before it disappears.

E—Extend the Legacy

Wealth multiplies when it outlives you. Build with the long term in mind. Give with structure and intention, teach what you have learned, and create systems people can carry forward.

What the ELITE Principles Actually Ask of You

They ask for honesty about where you are, what you believe, and what you're willing to do differently. They don't require perfection, a certain income level, or the right starting point. They ask for a clear look at your life and the courage to build from there.

Elevate asks you to stop running your financial life on beliefs that were handed to you by people who were also trying to survive.

Leverage asks you to stop underestimating the value you've already built through your experience, your story, and your skills.

Invest asks you to stop waiting for permission to let your money grow.

Tidy asks you to stop avoiding the numbers and start owning what's actually there.

Extend asks you to stop thinking that wealth is only for you, and to start building something that outlasts you.

None of this is easy. But none of it is out of reach, either.

Here's what we ask of you:

Pick one principle and put it into action within the next seven days. Don't wait for the perfect one or for better timing. Choose one and begin. Say it out loud, write it down, and tell someone who'll hold you to it. Wealth grows when action is followed by accountability.

Begin. Build. And then keep going.

Stay in the Community

Reading this book is only the beginning. Through Seeds4Wealth, we're building a community of first generation wealth builders who are done waiting for permission and ready to build something real.

Join the community, access tools that go deeper into the ELITE Principles, and connect with others on the same journey at www.seeds4wealth.org.

If you'd like to support the work of making financial education accessible to under-resourced students and communities, you can do that there as well. Every contribution helps extend the reach of what this book began.

Bring *EARNED* to Your Institution

The financial education gap that this book addresses doesn't stop at the individual. It lives inside schools, workforce programs, and career colleges where students arrive motivated to change their lives but leave without the financial foundation to sustain it.

EARNED for Education was built for exactly that gap. It's a turnkey financial literacy program designed to integrate into orientation, first-year experience, or career preparation courses without adding instructional burden to faculty. Schools that have implemented structured financial education programs see measurable improvements in student persistence, completion rates, and post-graduation financial stability. EARNED for Education is built to deliver those outcomes.

The program equips students to understand the real cost and return on their education, navigate financial aid with clarity, use every campus resource to their financial advantage, and build the money habits that last beyond graduation. It's not a personal finance elective. It's a retention tool that pays for itself.

If you lead an institution that wants to do more than simply enroll students, and if you truly want to actually equip them for what comes next, we'd like to talk. Reach out at info@seeds4wealth.org or visit www.seeds4wealth.org to start the conversation.

About the Authors

Duemand L. Edwards

Few people have spent more than two decades at the intersection of education, enterprise, and economic transformation — not as an observer, but as the person running the institution, building the organization, and making the decisions that determine whether people rise or stay stuck.

He grew up the youngest of eleven children in a household where financial education didn't exist, and economic survival was the only framework available. That origin didn't produce a victim. It produced a relentless student of why some people escape that cycle and most don't — and a practitioner who has spent a career doing something about it.

Edwards has led multi-campus healthcare education institutions at the executive level, overseeing hundreds of millions in annual revenue, complex regulatory environments, and the kind of organizational cultures that either produce outcomes or quietly kill them. He has operated at the VP, EVP, and President level across some of the most demanding environments in American higher education — building teams, turning around campuses, and holding the line on both performance and accountability when the two were in conflict.

He is the co-founder and Board President of Seeds4Wealth — a movement built on the conviction that poverty ends when people are given real financial education, not charity. Seeds4Wealth operates at the intersection of wealth literacy, community transformation, and direct human need, delivering programs that address financial independence alongside essentials like food and clothing security. Its reach extends internationally, including the founding and construction of an accredited school in Guyana — built from the ground up as a direct expression of the organization's mission to make economic opportunity structural, not occasional.

He also leads VestaLinx, a business education consulting firm that works with entrepreneurs and organizations to turn ideas into viable ventures and elevate existing operations to their full potential — through coaching, training, business model evaluation, and curriculum design built for real-world applications.

What qualifies Duemand Edwards to write this book is not a credential or a title. It is the fact that he has sat across from thousands of intelligent, hardworking people who were losing — and he understood exactly why. The ELITE Framework™ did not come from a classroom. It came from watching real people make Survival Decisions in real time and deciding that the pattern had to stop.

EARNED is that decision in book form.

Learn more at www.seeds4wealth.org.

Robert T. Vaughn

Few people have built a career that spans the boardrooms of Fortune 500-level financial institutions, the front lines of urban workforce transformation, and the infrastructure of organizations designed to pull entire communities out of poverty — and done all three with the same level of conviction.

Vaughn grew up in Chicago's inner city, where scarcity wasn't a concept — it was the daily operating condition. He attended public schools, experienced bankruptcy firsthand, and came face to face with every circumstance this book describes. He didn't write about Survival Decisions from a distance. He lived them — and then systematically dismantled them.

What followed is a career that most people would struggle to categorize. Vaughn has served as a Global Chief Information Security Officer, a Deputy CISO at a major financial institution, and a technology executive across some of the most complex and high-stakes environments in American enterprise. He spent nearly a decade building and protecting the kind of digital infrastructure that corporations and governments depend on — and then turned that same system-level thinking toward a different problem entirely.

As Chief Innovation Officer at NPower — one of the nation's leading nonprofit technology training organizations — Vaughn has spent years doing what this book argues is the only real answer to generational poverty: giving people the skills, credentials, and connections that create actual economic mobility. Not inspiration. Infrastructure.

He is the co-founder of Seeds4Wealth and co-creator of the ELITE Framework™ — built alongside Duemand Edwards on the shared belief that wealth is not a matter of luck, income, or even intelligence. It is a matter of decisions. And decisions can be taught.

What Robert Vaughn brings to EARNED is the proof of concept. He is the living argument that the distance between bankruptcy and building something that matters is not talent, not timing, and not circumstance. It is a framework — applied relentlessly over time.

EARNED is that framework.

www.ingramcontent.com/pod-product-compliance
Lightning Source LLC
LaVergne TN
LVHW022109200926
848481LV00003B/1117